The Grand Louvre's Pyramid

Texts by
Joël Girard and Guy Boyer
Translated by Benjamin Ivry

An Entrance Worthy of a Palace

EIGHT CENTURIES AND ANY NUMBER OF ARCHITECTS WERE NEEDED TO BUILD THE LOUVRE. LITTLE BY LITTLE, THE MUSEUM TOOK OVER THE PALACE'S TERRITORY. THE PYRAMID IS THE LATEST ARRIVAL ON THE SCENE.

The Louvre has had a fantastic, unique destiny. First it was the heart of France's Royal capital, later of the Republic. Its complex history is that of the nation. Its architecture weds great artistic and historical currents. There have been a sum total of no less than eight centuries of projects, constructions, repairs, and demolitions. During these eight centuries its uses have metamorphozed in equally surprising ways. After being the royal residence ; it was turned into the headquarters for the Revolutionary Comité de Salut public, responsible for so many executions of royalists. The Louvre has been a place for public celebrations as well as a prison. And finally, of course, in perhaps its best-known guise, as a modern-day museum. It is a melting pot, a place where memories meet, blending the styles of the Renaissance and classicissm, the Crown and the Republic. The Louvre's origins date back some eight hundred years to the reign of King Philippe-Auguste. The latter ordered the construction, not of a palace, but of a stronghold in the north of Paris.

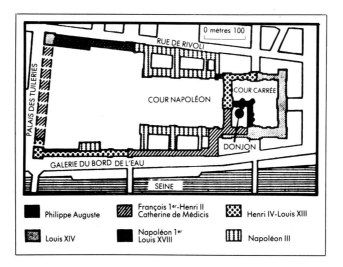

At the time the capital city was grouped into two main quarters — the City (the islands, now known as the Ile de la Cité and the Ile Saint-Louis) and the University (what we call the left bank, or *rive gauche*).
As a city in expansion, medieval Paris needed to be protected by a bridgehead that was well fortified on the right bank. The chosen spot was called « Lupara », which came to be called « Louvre ». Trenches were dug, walls and watchpaths were built. The medieval citadel was constructed. Today important vestiges of it remain under the Cour Carrée, notably the castle-keep that held the archives, the treasury, and the royal furniture repository. A castle-keep thirty meters high acted as a symbol for the fiefs that were attached to the royalty. King Philippe-Auguste's work marked the expansion of the city's right bank and symbolized a power seeking to affirm itself. After that, the Louvre's development would operate along a parallel course with the kingdom's consolidation. Saint Louis had a large room built in the castle. It was there that Saint-

This lithograph by Charles Rivière after a photograph of 1860, shows the symmetry of the Louvre buildings and their way of closing in around the Carrousel. On the lower level, the Tuileries, which join the pavillon de Flore to the pavillon de Marsan. These two are the only ones that remain in existence today. (Previous page. Photo Arthus-Bertrand/Explorer. To the left, photo D.R. Opposite, photo Viollet.)

Louis's crypt was brought, and where the archeological discoveries from the digs under the Cour Carrée are displayed. Charles V's architect, Raymond du Temple, enlarged and equipped the extant buildings in the 1360s. Moreover, King Charles V installed his library there. The Louvre fortress became a royal residence ; even if the Palais de la cité remained the official residence. Kings until the epoch of Henri II stayed there only irregularly. The illustrations of the « Très Riches Heures du duc de Berry » provide evidence of the history and architecture of the Louvre at the time of Charles V.

But the kingdom was still fragile. So vulnerable in fact that the Louvre during the Capetian era saw its development stopped by the Hundred Year's War. Victorious, the English occupied Paris. King Henry V of England, quite illegally proclaimed the King of France, and the Duke of Bedford, named English Regent in France, lived in the Louvre during the fifteenth century. This hiatus continued with the Valois' disdain for Paris and their passion for

the Loire Valley. So, in the fifteenth century the Louvre fortress served as a depot for armaments and artillery. It was also the headquarters for certain royal administrators. During their stays in Paris, the Kings of France preferred to stay at the Hôtel de Tournelles, which was more pleasant and less austere. For at the time the Louvre was still a medieval fortress, not exactly comfortable. King François I, in calling the Court to the Louvre, would be the first to use it as a palace.

As the imperatives of defense and security were lessened, the « fat tower » was razed, that had been the castle-keep for Philippe-Auguste. The moats that had been dug to isolate the base of the castle-keep were filled in, as well. François I no longer had any need for these signs of feudality. His legitimacy and sovereignty were no longer contested. The Royal Patron opted to build a completely new section, and named an architect, Pierre Lescot, who was a friend of the poet Ronsard, to design it. The sculptor Jean Goujon was designated to decorate it, in order to

Important Dates

From Charles V's Louvre, seen here in an illumination from the «Très Riches Heures » of Jean, duc de Berry, to the Cour Carrée of the 17th century, the buildings changed from medieval fortress to classical palace. In turn, they were redecorated and enlarged once again in the 19th century. (To the left, photo Giraudon. Below, photo RMN).

12th and 13th century Founding of the Louvre by King Philippe Auguste and by Saint Louis. 14th century. Charles V enlarges the castle and installs his personal library there.

1527-1530 King François I has the castle-keep and west wing of the old Louvre demolished. The architect Pierre Lescot has the task of rebuilding the Louvre.

1564-1570 Catherine de Médicis has a château in the Tuileries.

1624 Louis XIII announces his « great plan, » to make a vast royal space from the Cour Carrée to the Tuileries, linked by a « gallery alongside the riverbank. »

1653 King Louis XIV calls Le Vau to the Louvre. The Cour Carrée is to be enclosed.

1667-1670 The architects Le Vau, Perrault, and d'Orbay build the Colonnade.

1678 Louis XIV leaves for the château de Versailles.

1791 The National Assembly decides to establish a museum in the Grande Galerie of the Louvre.

1793 The Convention founds the Louvre Museum.

1806-1824 Fontaine and Percier, construct the Arc de triomphe of the Carrousel. They add some refurbishings of the northern part of the Louvre.

1852-1880 Lefuel and Visconti complete the « great plan » of Louis XIII.

1882-1883 The Tuileries burned in 1871, are demolished.

1905 The Musée des Arts Décoratifs is opened, rue de Rivoli.

1938 Redecoration of the Grande Galerie.

1968 The Ministry of Finances decides to leave the Pavillon de Flore.

1981 François Mitterrand, as President of the Republic, decides to install the « Grand Louvre » in the totality of the palace.

1989 Opening of the Pyramid designed by I.M. Pei. □

In the 19th century, the architects Fontaine and Percier constructed the triumphal arch of the Carrousel. The north wing, the symmetry of the Grande Galerie and the redecoration of the Tuileries palace. Visconti and Lefuel enlarged the Louvre around the Napoleonic Courtyard, opening the gates and opening the palace itself to the urban life around it. (Photo Roger-Viollet.)

make a palace worthy of that name and worthy of a King who was a great art-lover. Inspired by the art of Italy, the palace's eastern part offered an entrance which became the main entryway. The royal apartments, installed on the side of the Seine River, benefitted from an extraordinarily exposed site. Most of the medieval towers along the banks of the River were razed. The totality designed by Lescot has a classical sense of order. The casements were enlarged, and the windowglass colored. Numerous apartments were furnished to house a court that became more and more important.

This court was nearby, and dependent on its King. Thanks to the superb constructions of Lescot, François I was able to impress the great Charles the Fifth of Spain when he received him in 1540. The meeting took place in the new palace, proudly exhibiting on its facade the royal arms, sumptuously decorated for the occasion. After the death of François I, this ambitious restructuring that broke with the tradition of the Middle Ages, was continued by King Henri II, under the guidance of the same architect, Lescot. The western part of the palace was

redecorated, resulting in what would become the Cour Carrée. Thus the Valois Dynasty assured the continuity of this great project by furnishing the « Petite Galerie ». Henri II's wife, Catherine de Médicis, was responsible for expanding the Louvre towards the west. She ordered a new palace at the place called The Tuileries, from the architects Philibert Delorme and Jean Bullant. A central pavillion and two galleries were built.

In 1610, the body of King Henri IV, assassinated on the rue de la Ferronnerie was brought to the « galery alongside the water », the current site for the Grande Galerie. The gallery linked the Cour Carrée with the château des Tuileries.

Henri's widow, Marie de Médicis, shied away from the Louvre thereafter. She had the Palais du Luxembourg built for herself (now the home of the French Senate). Louis XIII was not a true lover of the Louvre either. When he died, Anne of Austria preferred to move to the Palais Cardinal (what we know as the Palais Royal), which had been bequeathed by Richelieu. When the Fronde arrived, she was dislocated rather abruptly moved with the future Louis XIV. The latter, marked by this episode, hired the architect Lemercier ; starting in 1652. Thirty years before, Lemercier had built the Pavillon de l'Horloge, now called the Pavillon Sully. Louis also commissioned the painters Lebrun and Le Sueur to decorate the apartments of the Queen. In 1659 Le Vau and the Vigaranis completed the « Salle des Machines ». The Petite Galerie (also called the Galerie d'Apollon) was refurbished by Le Vau and Lebrun. But the Minister Colbert did not appreciate the architecture of what would be the Institut de France, located on the left bank, facing the Cour Carrée. So, to avoid hiring Le Vau for the job, Colbert launched an international « competition for ideas » in order to continue the extension of the Louvre palace.

Foreigners like the Italian Bernini, then at the height of his glory, were invited to Paris to submit their projects. Then Colbert found that he did not agree with Bernini's ideas either, and the Italian's propositions were refused. Finally, the Sun-King would choose a project by a French architect who was also a man of science and a doctor. Claude Perrault was

called upon to build a monumental, classical colonnade to the east, facing Saint-Germain-l'Auxerrois. Le Vau's loss of prestige was only temporary, and limited to Paris. He would shortly become the director of a project equally ambitious in its own way : Versailles. This splendid commission would in a certain way constitute his revenge after the failure at the Louvre. In 1662 a « Carrousel » was took place between the Louvre and the Tuileries by Louis XIV, on the occasion of the birth of the Grand Dauphin. This great display would give its name to the place where it was performed.

In any event, for over a century, the King, his court and government would reside at Versailles. The Louvre's gardens were replanned by Le Nôtre. But these plans were allowed to drop and remained incompleted, in a perpetual state of construction. Numerous buildings were left without roofs. Moreover, the Louvre was assigned the role of the King's storehouses, and given over to administrators who were neither respectful nor overscrupulous about the place. When the Revolution broke out, Parisians brought the Royal Family to

The Napoleonic Courtyard is the heart of the Louvre. The Richelieu Wing contains the duc de Morny's apartments, where the Ministry of Finance's services were installed. The salons will be opened to the public and will adjoin the department of Objets d'Art. (D.R.)

a Louvre that was still under construction. Considered as a symbol of the Ancien Régime, it was not spared the Revolutionary fever. Thus, in 1793, the Convention decreed that all attributes of royalty should be destroyed at the Louvre and the Tuileries. From then on, the Palace belonged to the People.

The Convention decided the change in function of this royal collectivity : that it should go to the People, that the royal collections of paintings henceforth be open to the masses, and that the Louvre become a museum. In 1793 the Louvre Museum was officially opened. The last great architectural development for the Louvre came in the nineteenth century. The first Empire completed the great quadrilateral. Percier and Fontaine constructed the north wing symmetrical with the Grande Galerie. Also added were the triumphal arch of the Carrousel and redecoration of the palais des Tuileries.

The Second Empire attempted to realize the dream, by now many centuries old, of a « Grand Louvre », by linking the old Louvre with the Tuileries. Haussmann had had the entire residential quarter situated between the two palaces demolished. Thus, Visconti and Lefuel were able to build their constructions here and there around the Napoleonic Court : The Pavillon de Rohan and the buildings on the place du Palais-Royal, the pavillon de La Trémoille, the triple guichet of the Carrousel, and the conference room.

Just when it seemed as if the great plan had been finally completed, the Commune burned the Tuileries down, in 1871. The Tuileries were demolished completely ten years later, by order of the National Assembly. The unity of the ensemble seemed irreperably lost. Yet at the same time, a powerful perspective was established, opening up the Louvre to its exterior, a perspective going from east to west towards the Concorde and l'Etoile.

Now the Convention's declaration that the Louvre should be a museum belonging to all has been renewed. Museological aims will benefit from this powerful place in the human memory. It is only now that we have created a main entrance to the entire system of buildings, so vast, that stretch out for nearly a kilometer. □

*T*he project of the Grand Louvre will re-center the collections towards the east of the building. The northern wing is still occupied by the Central Union of Decorative Arts. The other wing, to the south, is transformed into offices, all the while saving the pavillon de Flore for the Department of Graphic Arts. (Photo Marc Garanger.)

One Thousand Days of Construction

I n the fall of 1981, François Mitterrand, the President of the Republic, decided to make the Louvre into the « greatest museum in the world ». The project was an ambitious one, or, as its detractors put it, « pharaonic ». However, the great construction site that has been entrusted to the Chinese-American architect Ieoh Ming Pei, is only the logical end of a very old museological process. The Louvre Pyramid symbolizes this project ; perhaps that is why it in particular has unleashed a series of passionate reactions from supporters and opponents alike.

By a decree dated May 26, 1791, the revolutionary forces decided that the royal collection of art should be in principle open to the public. This proclamation can be seen as the birth of the modern museum. As such, the Louvre Museum opened its doors in 1793. However, the use of the Louvre as an artistic center and even as a museum dates back to the Ancien Régime, before the Revolution. King Henri IV was the first to authorize artists to occupy the palace. The artists would remain lodged there, more or less, until the nineteenth century. Louis XIV, the Sun-King, installed Academies of painting, sculpture, and architecture there. The Louvre became the site for these acade-

mies' annual exhibitions. Louis XIV also charged the painter Charles Lebrun with organizing the gallery of the King's paintings. Lebrun was also asked to present the models of the fortified cities of France in the Grande Galerie. The actuel idea of the Museum came from the Count d'Angivillier, Director General of the King's Buildings, as well as from the architect Soufflot.. This monarchical origin of the Museum is personified by the painter Hubert Robert. Robert started out as the guardian of the King's paintings. He next became one of the curators of the Museum begun by the Revolutionary Convention and the painter Jacques-Louis David.

Moreover, since the beginning of the eighteenth century, certain departments, notably the collection of drawings' had already been open to the public.

Since the time of King François I, the Museum's collections underwent important changes. These were most dramatic during the Napoleonic cam-

1905. The last museographic extension of the Louvre dates back to 1968, when the Ministry of Finances left the Pavillon de Flore. It would not be until the end of the 1970s that the Louvre would be the subject of a museographic project worthy of its collections, that would respond at the same time to the

After two years of digging, the construction could begin. Day by day an electronic camera photographed the evolution of the work. To the left, in August 1985, the archeologists disengaged the bedrock of ancient constructions. To the right, in April 1987, the infrastructures of the Pyramid were already in place. (Preceding pages, photos L. Boegly / Archipress. Opposite, photo P. Astier / EPGL.)

paigns ; Bonaparte was not only a conquering general, he was also an avid art collector, and vast amounts of booty filled the Louvre during the time of his successful battles. In 1817, the already existing Museum of French Monuments closed its doors, and its sculptures were transferred over to the collections of the Louvre. Plus, in the nineteenth century, many antique works were added as well. Little by little all of these collections began to fill the four wings of the Cour Carrée. The Musée de la Marine stayed for some time on the premises of the Louvre. The Ecole du Louvre was founded in 1882, and the Musée des Arts Décoratifs was established in

needs of a new museum-going public, in the same tradition as American museums before had adapted to the modern era. Thus, the project of the « Grand Louvre ». For if the sum total of the buildings had acquired with time a certain architectural cohesion, the same was not true of the museum. It had been installed in a disorderly manner in a palace that had been originally conceived with concerns completely foreign to museography.

The idea of the Grand Louvre consisted in reorganizing the museum into one compact unit, to enlarge the surfaces available for exhibitions, to redeploy the collections, now presented in a more logi-

Opposite, in December 1987, the flagging of the outer area of the Napoleonic Courtyard is a work in progress. The metallic structures of the Pyramid are already finished. They only await the emplacement of special glass that has been developped in order to ensure the maximum transparency. To the right ; in October 1988, the Napoleonic Courtyard has just been opened to the public. (Photos Patrice Astier / EPGL.)

cal fashion and with more breathing room in the totality of buildings. Finally, the aim was to bestow upon the Museum all of the necessary infrastructures for the conservation and the preservation of the works, as well as for the reception of visitors. The redeployment of the collections was made possible by the scheduled departure of the Ministry of Finances from the Richelieu Wing on the rue de Rivoli. These offices will move to a smart new building in the suburb of Bercy. This decision was saluted in an almost unanimous fashion as « *courageous... a decision that should have been made long ago* ».

However, the palatial nature of the space's design and its doubly long-limbed composition required the invention of new areas. Only the spaces in the cellars beneath the Napoleonic Courtyard were free. It was there that the heart of the Museum would be located. Such was the challenge taken up by the American architect of Chinese background,

Ieoh Ming Pei. Pei was named without any competition in March 1983 by the President François Mitterrand. « *A royalist deed* », said opponents to the project. Even the Minister of Culture, Jack Lang, had to concede that it was a « *despotic signing* ».

Im Pei's set architectural purpose shocked a number of people, and set into motion a flood of opposition. No one attempts to disagree with the usefulness of the planned installations, but apart from the project's cost, Pei is reproached for wanting to build a pyramid. A pyramid of glass, more than twenty meters high, at the heart of this historic site considered by certain critics as « *finished* » and already « *saturated with architecture and history* ». True, the accumulations of styles was enough to paralyse more than one architectural imagination. The polemics forced the craftsmen and the architect to make a model in May 1985, in life size, as was once done with the Arc de Triomphe. Already, the « false pyramid » captivated the glances of the curious. Some rejected it because it was transparent. Others, praising its transparency, nevertheless refused any new addition to the site. On the other land, there was the ever-present question of cleaning. Emile Biasini, the Secretary of State for great works, replied, « *It's a question of housekeeping* ». Pei and his collaborators, the architectural firm of Macary and Duval, hoped to make a modern museum in the heart of the palace. They planned to make a vital, welcoming space all the while preserving the history of the place. Pei, the architect

of the new building for the National Gallery in Washington, D.C., managed nonetheless to impose his pyramid, a transparent, reflecting prism.

The pyramid does not mask the old edifice, or the perspectives. It only blocks already obstructed views, composes a central point and a crossing as well. The ensemble, very much composed of stone materials, is enthroned in the center of seven triangular basins of deep blue granite. Three « pyramidions » placed in the directions of the Sully, Richelieu, and Denon pavillons, mark the three entrances to the guided tours. These smaller pyra-

mids also admit light to the underground galleries. The great pyramid makes up the main entrance to the museum. It is the sign of a more compact unity. I.M. Pei's idea was nothing if not a hardy one. For him, the Louvre had to become a living link between the Left Bank and the Right Bank of the Seine River. This reconciliation of the two sides of Paris is personified by a giant parvis, a vast open « plazza » in the Italian tradition, open day and night. Pedestrian traffic will give life to this place previously occupied by Ministry automobiles.

Underneath the pyramid, Pei created in around twelve acres, a totality of infrastructures that are indispensable to the new Museum. This arrangement came about after the underground area had been emptied to the depth of nine meters, through very detailed digs. The glass pyramid inundates a gigantic welcoming space with light. Visitors will have access to this space either from the underground parking lots, or through the Napoleonic Courtyard, or also through the metro station, via the Richelieu passage.

Until the present time, the Museum included 246 galleries over some 30,000 square meters, but without presenting its collections in any coherent, chronologic order. Taking into account all of the buildings, with the exception of those that will still be used by the Arts décoratifs, the Museum can display its collections over 50,000 square meters, or almost double the exposition surface that was available before the construction began.

The Grand Louvre, so long awaited by curators and the general public, delayed by political squabbles, will at last see a conclusion. Begun in 1981, it will be definitively ended with the underground parking lots, the sales galleries, and the refurbishing of the Tuileries gardens. All of these final touches will take place, it is projected, by 1995. □

In October 1988, President François Mitterrand, accompanied by Prime Minister Michel Rocard and Cultural Minister Jack Lang, dedicate the Pyramid and the Napoleonic Courtyard. The fireworks of a sound-and-light show embrace the Louvre with the red, white and blue colors of France. It is fitting that the tricolored flag should thus be evoked in this bicentennial year of the French Revolution. (Photo by N'Diaye / Imapress.)

*Preceding page. Through the Arc du Carrousel
(photo N'Diaye / Imapress). To the left. View of
the Richelieu passage (Couturier / Archipress).*

*Above. The mountain climber-glass-cleaners
(photo S. Sautereau). Following pages, the Napoleonic Courtyard (photo A. Wolf / Explorer).*

To the left, the helical stairway (photo Stéphane Couturier / Archipress). Above, the metallic structure of the Pyramid (photo Serge Sautereau).

Following page. Underneath the Pyramid, a vast hall points the visitor in three important directions : Sully, Denon, and Richelieu. (Photo A. Wolf / Explorer).

Above. The perfect curve of an interior stairway (photo S. Sautereau). To the right. When concrete allies with glass (photo S. Couturier / Archipress).

Double Page Following. At nightfall, the basins around the Pyramid become colored with the colors of evening (photo N'Diaye / Imapress).

Above. At night from the top of the Sully Pavillon, the off-centered axis of the Défense-Etoile-Carrousel-Louvre can be seen. (Photo Serge Sautereau.)

Following page. The Pyramid. The sole entrance to the Grand Louvre and new symbol of the Museum, is surrounded by « pyramidions ». (Photo Serge Sautereau.)

Bernini's Revenge

Gian Lorenzo Bernini, great master of the baroque, had been contacted to « *put on paper a few of those admirable thoughts that are so familiar to you and of which you have given so many demonstrations* ». Bernini sent two successive projects for the enlargement of the Louvre to Louis XIV. These drawings had a somewhat revolutionary character. The Sun-King's powerful Minister, Colbert, asked the famous Italian architect to come to France. At the more sight of these projects, the objections rained down immediately, criticizing the interior disposition of the rooms, the absence of fortifications, the terraces unsuitable for the Parisian climate, etc. Despite the architect's best efforts, the project was abandoned in 1666. The crafty Colbert claimed that there were financial problems, allied to the war currently going on. As a consolation prize, Bernini was given a commission for a great equestrian statue in marble of the Sun-King. But the King didn't find that sculpture to his taste, either, and it was banished to the end of the piece d'eau des Suisses at Versailles.

More than three centuries later, can we go back and rehabilitate an architect at the Louvre who was as decisivelt blackballed as Bernini ? The baroque master was defeated by the tenets of French classicism, permanently, it would seem. To try to do so would require more than a little tenacity, or perhaps a little cynicism as well. In the Grand Louvre, I.M. Pei insisted that a lead copy of Bernini's sculpture of the

Copy in lead of a marble original by Bernini. The equestrian statue of Louis XIV will enthrone the end of the great perspective Louvre-Concorde-Défense. Can it be seen as a sign of the artist's revenge ?

Sun-King be placed at the end of the great perspective of the Louvre-Carrousel-Etoile. In the final choice of Bernini's work, we may see the handwritting of I.M. Pei, who may in a sense be responding to the French architects who opposed his own project. For better than Bernini in this sense, Ieoh Ming Pei knew extremely well how to go about imposing his vision of architecture on the Louvre, which in our time was the Louvre of the architects Lefuel and Visconti.

But this arrangement posed what came to be seen as a double problem. The Italian master's work was intended to be marble. How could a casting in lead be acceptable, which resembled modeling clay ? And above all, why place at the axis of a faraway perspective a sculpture that was conceived to be seen in all of its imposing size ? Today, this copy stares out at the salons of the duc de Morny, the former location of the Ministry of Finance. Bernini was retained, and not just for the space beneath the pyramid, which would have been the logical solution, but for its exterior, highly visible and even symbolic site. Under the pyramid it certainly would have been more in its place. Michel Guy foresaw as much at one point, confronting the Colonnade designed by the trio of classicists Perrault-Le Vau-d'Orbay.□

Some Statistics

— Seven months of computer calculations in order to arrive at the precise structure of the building, and its 150,000 assembly points.
— Three years of construction.
— 21.6 m high, 35 m wide.
— 612 lozenges of glass - each 3 meters by 1.90 meters - weighing 150 kilograms apiece.
— The weight of the Pyramid structure amounts to 180 tons.
— 966 floodlights brighten the Pyramid's interior.
— A sum total of 86 tons of glass.

This construction site, three years in the making, for a monumental building necessitated enormous financial, technological, and human contributions. On the left, an original method of cleaning by mountain climbers. (Photo N'Diaye / Imapress.) Below, an aerial view of the glass tetrahedron. (Photo Yann Arthus-Bertrand / Explorer.) Right, the metal network supporting the 86 tons of glass. (Photo S. Sautereau.)

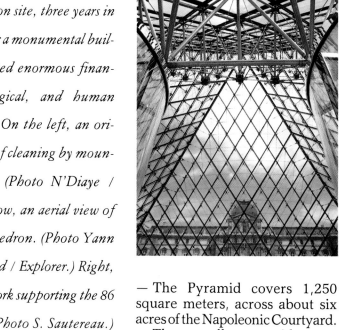

— The Pyramid covers 1,250 square meters, across about six acres of the Napoleonic Courtyard.
— Three smaller pyramids, measuring eight meters at their bases and five meters in height.
— Cost of the pyramid : 75 million francs. The structure, including underground areas, drains, and the esplanade, cost two billion francs.
— Three billion more francs will also be spent, after the Ministry's departure, to rearrange the display of the collections.
— 650,000 paving stones of sandstone and granite for the parvis.
— Twelve acres of constructions underneath the Pyramid.
— The 70.000 square meters of the museum will make it the largest in the world.
— Nearly 30.000 artworks will be presented.
— More than 5.000.000 visitors are expected every year.
— September, 1981 : when the project began.
— 1995, completion of the project.

A Full Menu of Equipment

STOREROOMS, LABORATORIES,
AN AUDITORIUM, AN IMMENSE
BOOKSTORE, RESTAURANTS, BOUTIQUES,
AND RECEPTION SERVICES FILL OUT
THE SPACE «UNDER THE PYRAMID».

T he pyramid marks the center of an apparatus destined to facilitate traffic and visits from one section of the museum to another. It offers shelter to reception areas and places for new activities. The sophistication and abundance of these areas create a diversion in themselves. Some pessimists claim that these virtues distract visitors from the essential point, that is, the works of art themselves. For the defenders of the project, first and foremost the Museum curators themselves, they are accessory spaces utterly necessary for any modern museum that hopes to attract the largest possible public.

All of the entrances to the Museum converge by elevators and escalators towards the space beneath the pyramid. Brilliantly lit, it is a meeting place, an information center, a place where tours begin, and also a resting spot. Once a visitor enters the Napoleonic Hall, nine meters beneath the courtyard, all of the polemics vanish from the mind. In fact, the pyramid offers a truly fantastic vision of lthe Louvre of the nineteenth century. The public can find all sorts of useful commodities in this gigantic hall, surrounded by a mezzanine : at last, sufficient coat-checking facilities, and places to check sacks and parcels, a post office, money-changing counters, travel agencies, rest rooms... Here the visit to the Museum is prepared. Entrance to the different departments, to special shows and current activi-

S everal escalators take people from the Napoleonic Courtyard to the space under the Pyramid. The most spectacular of these must be the stairway in the shape of a helix that surrounds the elevator that works by pistons. (Previous page and above. Photo Stéphane Couturier / Archipress.) The three great guided tours that leave from the Hall have been named after the pavillions that they visit : Sully, Richelieu, and Denon.

An Exceptional Realization

The architect I.M. Pei, assisted by his colleagues and engineers, envisioned a perfectly planar pyramid. They saw it as having a light, elegant structure. The structure was to be as light as a spider's web. The original idea, as well as the realization of the building, the putting together of an entity with construction materials and techniques, constituted a technological performance. It was necessary to resort to studies by research groups and to artificial intelligence. Seven months of computer studies were carried out. The businesses involved pursued further research. Saint-Gobain Glassworks consecrated two years of study to arrive at a product that is unique in its genre, a «special clear glass. » Containing less ferrous oxide, it is less green than other glasses, almost entirely white. Baked in a special oven using electric fusion, it offers suppleness and lightness.

This layered glass of 2;15 centimeters thickness offers great transparency, despite the weight of the ensemble, a total of eighty-six tons. The French Company for Metalurgic Enterprises in mastering the work for the metallic structure, ended up with a rust-proof steel framework weighing ninety-five tons. They were inspired by the techniques of constructing racing ships. Divided into lozenges, the structure is held together by an interior ribbing system and with counter-cables, like the guys of ships. The thin structure, or chassis, made of a mixture of lacquered aluminium, consists of no less than six thousand individual elements. The

———————◆———————

It was necessary to call upon the highest levels of technology to conceive and complete the pyramid and its trappings. To the left, the cables that support the tension of the system. To the right, the putting into place of some 666 lozenges of glass. (Photo on the left. S. Sautereau. On the right. A. Wolf / Explorer.)

———————◆———————

putting together of the building on the site required great meticulousness. The purity of the structure's lines and the planar qualities of its surfaces were dependent on the perfection of its joints, solderings, and other fastenings. The glass was put into place by workers in cars equipped with vents. A sophisticated operation. The six hundred and sixty six windows, each weighing 150 kg, are affixed to the metal by a silicone cement developped by the Rhone-Poulenc Company.

But performances are not limited to the pyramid. In the Hall, the most astonishing element is the Otis Elevator, at the heart of the helical stairway. Under the pyramid, the quality of the concrete is remarkable. The Dumez Company produced the pyramid-shaped coffered ceilings, from architectonic white concrete. The concrete was cast in Oregon pine parquet, using lathe framings. A costly product, but one that gives an exceptional result.

The technology also includes the use of artisanal methods, particularly for the cleaning of the pyramid, handled by a group of mountaineers. □

*A*n auditorium with 430 seats is located at the west of the Napoleonic Hall. Apart from lectures and colloquiums, it will also program concerts and recitals. (Photo Serge Sautereau). Some meters away from the temporary exhibition galleries, bas-reliefs by Jean Goujon, formerly exhibited at the Ecole des Beaux-Arts in Paris, decorate the galleries on the history of the Louvre, designed by Peduzzi. (Photo S. Couturier / Archipress.)

To the east, twelve hundred square meters of space is devoted to temporary expositions drawn from the Museum's collections. It is also used for showing drawings, or new acquistions of the different departments.

The first of these temporary shows organized in this malleable space has been conceived by Jean-Michel Wilmotte, with the theme : the 2700 Donators to the Louvre, who have permitted the enrichment of its collections from 1793 until the present day. The rooms dedicated to the History of the Louvre are among the most spectacular of the novelties. Prepared by Pierre Quoniam under the direction of decorator Richard Peduzzi, this evocation retraces the evolution of the palace and of the Museum, through models and original works of art relating to the Museum itself. These permanent galleries are the perfect preparation for a visit to the medieval Louvre, located under the Cour Carrée. This site includes the archeologic crypt, the moats, and the castlekeep of King Philippe-Auguste.

Inspired by France's experience that began with the Musée d'Orsay, the organization of educational and cultural activities for all the public is a sizeable innovation for the Louvre. Seminars and pedagogic days permit teachers to prepare the visits of school groups. These groups can pass an entire

ties are indicated on gigantic panels, informative lists, electronic terminals, and a center for documentation. At the reception area, the sale of tickets, guides, the renting of audio-guides, and more specialized information in each department. Four rectilinear «streets» emerge from the hall underneath the pyramid, indicating other spaces in the directions they follow. There are three principal directions for visits : Sully, Richelieu, and Denon. To the west, a walkway created by I.M. Pei leads to the « Friends of the Louvre » boutique, the finance office, the Caisse nationale des Monuments historiques, and eventually to the parking areas and to the sales gallery placed under the Carrousel.

Some New Archeological Discoveries

On the occasion of the construction of the Pyramid, the archeological excavations took place in three different parts. Under the Cour Carrée, the ramparts and castle-keep of King Charles V and King Philippe-Auguste were found. (Above. Photo Patrice Astier/EPGL). Between the pavillon de Flore and the pavillon de Marsan were found most notably, Bernard Palissy's ovens. Also found were the exact sites of the Royal menageries and aviaries. (Center. Photo Anne-Marie Minvielle). In the Napoleonic Courtyard. The Department of Historical Monuments have formed a passageway between the entrance hall and the archeologic crypt. There the counterfort planned by Le Vau can be seen. (Below. Photo Sautereau.)

The Grand Louvre has permitted a dream to be realized that has captivated several generations of archeologists : to dig up a large urban space right in the middle of Paris, under the current sites of the Cour Carrée and the Napoleonic Courtyard. The operation was directed by Michel Fleury, President of the Fourth Section of the Ecole Pratique des Hautes Etudes. Professor Fleury led the digs under the Cour Carrée, while Yves de Kisch, Inspector General of Archeology, commanded the work on the Napoleonic Courtyard. The project cost 80 million francs. In the Cour Carrée, the counterforts and the castle-keep of King Charles V's Louvre were extricated in order to arrange an archeological crypt.

The archeologists went about a « detailed » dig, thanks to enormous resources both in manpower and resources. This model excavation permitted a vast harvest of historic and scientific information on the daily life and history of the area of the Louvre, from neolithic times until the nineteenth century. A large number of facts were collected about the urban landscape, animals, plants, and foods of different areas ; thousands of objects were disinterred, even the helmets of Charles VI and of the dauphin Louis. Another important discovery was the enamel and tile kilns as well as pots and original moulds belonging to Palissy.

The digs on the site of the Carrousel should bring an equal number of information that is archeologically fascinating. □

Near Philippe Auguste's donjon, the Saint-Louis crypt presents archeological discoveries made by Michel Fleury in the Cour Carrée. Helmets of Charles VI and the Dauphin are among the master-works. A raw concrete ceiling links the destroyed medieval vaults. Through what was once the moat of the medieval castle, one arrives to the Department of Egyptian Antiquities. (Photo Serge Sautereau.)

day at the Louvre. They will participate in workshops, slide-shows, visits, lectures, and a space is specially reserved for them on the mezzanine, with a room reserved for picnicking. Visitors may also take advantage of the workshops. The specialized personnel therein work with regard to artistic technique as well as the scientific analysis of the works in the collections of the Museum itself. This new kind of pedagogic Museum will propose a varied menu of lectures. There will be the general visits to certain departments, visits according to a single theme, or also the popular « one hour, one work of art, » for those constrained to the time — limits of a business lunch. This latter formula attracts a good number of people who work in the vicinity, between 12:30 and 1:30 pm. An auditorium, directly accessible from the Napoleonic Courtyard, will schedule a program of colloquiums, lectures with simultaneous translations, and days dedicated to provincial or foreign museums. There will also be study of museography and the history of art, and also film — and slide — shows, notably of audiovisual programs produced by the Museum's cultural services. To captivate a larger public, concerts, recitals, and chamber music will be regulaly programmed in the auditorium. (see the last page for

more information on this subject).

The Grand Louvre proposes a variety of activities from many disciplines. The Louvre will be a Museum « à la carte. » The idea will be to hook visitors who only expected to spend a hour or two there, and never return, into wanting to return again and again. The Museum will become many-faced and alive. It will expose art, it will also expose itself, so to speak, as well as animating and educating its visitors. Thanks to all these activities, the bookstore, cafés, restaurants, and giftshops, the visitor can plan an entire day at the Louvre.

To be sure, the largest Museum in the world needed space for its storerooms as well as for administration, personnel, restoration workshops, and laboratories. All of these are located underneath the Napoleonic Courtyard, connected by a complex system of corridors and hallways leading from one to another. Sometime before 1993, the Museum's bicentennial, a second commercial gallery will be added and parking lots too, that will be directly accessible from the avenue Lemonnier and connected to the space beneath the Pyramid. The Louvre Museum will be one of the principal cultural attractions in Paris. Each year, six or seven million visitors are expected. □

Conversation with Ieoh Ming Pei

BEAUX-ARTS : Why did you accept to take charge of the project of the Grand Louvre ?
I.M. PEI : I hesitated for quite a while before finally accepting to participate in the realization of the Grand Louvre. I finally accepted because I felt that I could do a work of quality there and because good relations were established with Emile Biasini and with President Mitterrand.

B.-A. : Why did you opt for a symbolic representation for the only entrance ?
I.M. P. : The entrance by the Pyramid is the main entryway, but not the only one. You must understand that 75 per cent of the visitors to the Louvre are foreigners who need a single space for information, for checking their coats, etc. Parisians who know the Museum already, can always enter through other entrances, but these won't have all the same services.

B.-A. : Did you consider any other forms except the Pyramid ? And why did you choose to make out of glass ?
I.M. P. : As soon as we knew that we needed something to break the surface and to bring light and volume to an underground space, we looked for the most suitable form. We arrived at the Pyramid, after rejecting, for example, the dome, the cube, and the cone. Glass permits light to inundate the underground area, which can thus seem more ample. Without the glass pyramid, the whole thing would resemble a metro station. Moreover, thanks to the glass, it is possible to see the Lou-

Architecte Pei, commissioned directly by President François Mitterrand. (Photo Imapress.)

vre's facades from the subterranean level.

B.-A. : The Napoleonic Courtyard is already « *saturated with architecture* ». Isn't the Pyramid shocking for that already eclectic nineteenth century mixture ?
I.M. P. : It's true that the Napoleonic Courtyard has a very strong architectural presence. But it is not representative of the most glorious era of French architecture. The Pyramid and the basins that surround it constitute a mini-

malist geometric realization, closer to the spirit of Le Nôtre (the 17th century architect and landscape designer). I think that they are truly complimentary.

B.-A. : How do you conceive the modern museum ? What must it offer its public ?
I.M. P. : Today, the museum must respond to new preoccupations. In the last ten years, the number of visitors has augmented in a considerable fashion. And these visitors have less knowledge, about art, generally speaking. Thus we must propose new modes of visiting that are welcoming and comprehensible.

B.-A. : Don't you think that the imposing surface of the area underneath the Pyramid threatens to distract the public from the works of art themselves ?
I.M. P. : When you are alone in the Napoleonic Hall, it may seem vast. But it will be filled with people. In fact, it is exactly the same size as the entrace hall in the Metropolitan Museum of Art in New York. Because it is situated at the center of gravity of the Grand Louvre, it will on the contrary permit a more direct access to the exhibition spaces.

B.-A. : What lessons can be drawn from this experience in a place so marked by history and so dear to the French ?
I.M. P. : I grasp perfectly that the French are particularly attached to the Louvre. It is perhaps the most important architectural ensemble in France, at the heart of Paris. □

A Sophisticated Interior Decoration

Ieoh Ming Pei's architecture is monumental. However, the Napoleonic Hall and the new spaces present a generous freedom. Few materials are used, but they are offered in a noble, and finely honed manner of the highest quality. The universe of I.M. Pei is strict. He systematically has recourse to the square. But this universe is also welcoming and even reassuring, thanks to the vast pedestrian areas and the mezzanine as well. On the walls and floor, stones from Chassagne and Magny, noted quarry towns in France, are imbedded. Elsewhere, notably for the ceilings in sunken panels with a pyramidal form, a milky white concrete is used. Lightness, clarity, and rigour result. Plus, I.M. Pei has benefitted from the help of architect-designers for the realization of certain spaces : Richard Peduzzi and Jean-Michel Wilmotte.

Richard Peduzzi worked essentially in the historical galleries of the Museum. « *I was given two plain spaces, empty, narrow as corridors, with an unbelievable number of works and illustrations to present in them.* » Famous in the theatre, where he has worked on all of Patrice Chéreau's controversial productions, Peduzzi has also worked on the section of architecture and urbanism at the musée d'Orsay. There, it will be remembered, the visitor can walk over the glass that covers the model of the neighbourhood of the Paris Opera. « *Pei didn't want me to do the same thing that he did. So in the galleries, I installed a labyrinthine walk, just like the image that everyone has of the Louvre.* » The

visitor circles between the walls rather than the objects ; the walls, in inlaid wood, present the works and models realized like vertical plans in relief. To give some breathing space to these volumes, an opaline blue glass in suspended from above. The light it offers is diffuse, bluish. Projectors, which are not harsh, are directed on the documents presented in the glass cases. « *The space moves with the visitor. The interior architecture should be strong ; it should intrigue the passerby* », like a historical gar-

den. The link between museums and entertainment halls has long existed. Museums have caught a certain theatricality. But there seems to be a new switch possible, as well. Peduzzi states that the Louvre gave him some ideas for his next production of *Hamlet*.

In his forties, a designer, decorator, and architect, Jean-Michel Wilmotte is already well-known for his opera house in Nîmes, France, for the French Embassy in Washington, D.C., and for a « café-mass » in Tokyo. Emile Biasini and Ieoh Ming Pei called on him to conceptualize the decorations and furnishings of the bookstore, the boutique of engravings, the restaurants, and the galleries for temporary exhibitions. For example, for the specialized bookstore, Wilmotte created a specific furnishing, slanted and removeable. The racks for postcards, posters, books, and magazines, are made of unpainted maplewood, with a matte varnish, of metal in a colour known as « Pei grey », and of elements of sanded glass. A false stained-glass window attracts the visitor towards the upper level by a central stairway, in a squared shape, which helps to give structure to the two levels. Wilmotte's use of few materials, but including stone from the quarries of Chassagne, offers a certain classical restraint. If he is indeed classic, then Wilmotte is nonetheless audacious for all that. In the two parallel galleries for temporary exhibitions, the architecture itself is thought of in terms of museography. Ceilings and mouldings are removeable. The space can be modulated according to the occasion. □

Conversation with Emile Biasini

BEAUX-ARTS : Don't you regret giving the commission to Pei, without an open competition ?
EMILE BIASINI : Not at all. The results speak for themselves. I.M. Pei is one of the great architects of our time. He already has had a great deal of experience in the museum field. Pei is of Chinese origin, and perhaps for this reason he has a good understanding of the concept of tradition. He approached the project with profound respect.

B.A. : Yet Pei's contribution has received some criticism.
E.B. : The Pyramid has occasioned a certain number of polemics, but nothing that could stand up to the self-evident functional necessity and monumental value of the design. Pei has made a « shrouded architecture », as Boullée put it, without ever losing contact with what is outside. No matter what direction the museum-goers approach from, they can see the entrance to the Louvre with no ambiguity. This permanent visual contact guaranteed by the pyramid is Pei's real stroke of genius.

B.-A. : Has the project been modified since the Ministry of Finances agreed to leave the Richelieu wing of the Louvre ?
E.B. : President Mitterrand decided to give over to the Museum the part occupied by the Ministry of Finances since its origins. This administration is a powerful and old one. Putting Mr. Mitterrand's decision into effect was difficult. The period of cohabitation turned into a delay, but nothing was

---

Secretary of States for Great Works and the Bicentennial, Emile Biasini led the Grand Louvre project for five years as head of the Etablissement public du Grand Louvre. (Photo Bellavia / Rea.)

---

essentially modified in the Grand Louvre program. If the Ministry of Finances had not finally left, Pei's project would have been fatally compromised.

B.-A. : The Grand Louvre won't be finished until 1993 ; What are the steps that still have to occur ?
E.B. : On March 30, the Pyramid and two museum directions will be opened to the public. Two months more will be needed for preparing the Ministry of Finances' departure. After the Bicentennial of the French Revolution, we will start in once again by taking off the roof of the whole wing that will be free. Then the work on of the Richelieu wing can begin. Of the six levels, three will be kept, the courtyards will be covered, in order to contain sculptures.

B.-A. : Five billion francs, have been predicted as the cost. Will that be enough ?
E.B. : Yes. It's my job to watch over the expenses scrupulously. Two billion francs have been spent on the Pyramid, the Napoleonic Courtyard and the new underground spaces. A billion francs is forecast for the restoration of the whole of the building. Another billion francs goes for the restructuring of the Richelieu wing. Finally, another billion francs for the museological rearrangements and the surroundings of the Museum.

B.-A. : So the Grand Louvre will occupy the whole building from Saint-Germain-l'Auxerrois to the Tuileries.
E.B. : After the Napoleonic Courtyard has been refurbished, the courtyard of the Carrousel will also be reconstructed, as well as the terrace of the château des Tuileries. But apart from the terrace and the current buildings agreed on in a provisory way for the Bicentennial of the Revolution, the exact program has not yet been decided. But everyone agrees that the redesign of the Tuileries Gardens is necessary. □

Conversation with Michel Laclotte

BEAUX-ARTS : Why was the decision made to build the Grand Louvre ?

MICHEL LACLOTTE : The need to modernise the Louvre has been felt for a very long time. The collections were insufficiently presented or else presented in bad conditions. For the public, there had to be a better reception area. On the other hand, as it has often been said, the Louvre is a theater without wings. There was a real need for spaces devoted to technical matters. We lacked areas for storage, zones for stocking materials, and delivery points as well. A good number of these services were housed in really noble settings, such as the salle du Manège. The decision made by François Mitterrand, in 1981, resolved all these problems. We were accorded the areas occupied by the Ministry of Finances, representing in themselves the equivalent in space of the entire musée d'Orsay.

B.-A. : What did the architect bring to the project ?

M.L. : Pei found the way of enlarging the Museum without adding buildings onto it. We couldn't do that, because we are closed into a historic space. The key point was the idea of finding 80,000 square meters underground. Otherwise, we would have only been able to add the space occupied by the Ministry of Finances, enough to fill all of the functions we demanded of it. Pei's response was clear. The space installed underneath the Napoleonic Courtyard absorbs a great many of the technical needs. More space can be taken up by works

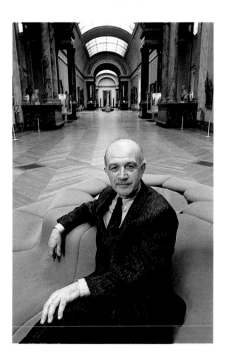

As Director of the Grand Louvre, Michel Laclotte spared no effort to redeploy the Museum's collections. Many new rooms opened at the end of march (Photo G. Uferas / Agence Vu.)

of art in the old buildings. Things are clearer also for the general public. Under the pyramid a very simple network of axes of pedestrian traffic in a cruciform shape.

B.-A. : Which departments and works will benefit from the transfer to the four levels of the Richelieu Wing?

M.L. : Four departments benefit directly from this extension. All the French sculpture will be presented in the Richelieu wing. At the bottom of the ground floor, there will be the section for Islamic art. On the top of the ground floor, Asian antiquities. The courtyards will be covered, and French sculpture will be displayed there. On the second floor, the department of objets d'art will extend right up to the Cour Carrée. On the top floor, will be the department of Northern paintings, that are currently badly housed. By the process of shifting, all the departments will benefit from a gain in space. In sum, we will gain about 80 per cent of extra space for exhibition. For the bicentennial of the Museum in 1993, we hope to open all four floors of the Richelieu wing.

B.-A. : What is the program of new cultural activities that the Museum proposes ?

M.L. : This will not be the musée d'Orsay. We have no intention of dealing with music, and literature from Babylon to Berlioz. But modern art will have a place at the Louvre.

B.-A. : Completing the Grand Louvre, would you say that the plan was a great adventure?

M.L. : I can say that it has been a great year in the history of the museum. There was a Revolution, which gave us the Museum to begin with. A second step was made during the Second Empire, when rebuilding went on. In my opinion we are experiencing the third great step. □

People and glasshouses...

« The President of the Republic, François Mitterrand, after having been informed of the propositions that were transmitted to him by the Ministry of Culture, has given his definite accord to the project for the Grand Louvre as presented by the architect I.M. Pei. **Communiqué from the Elysée, February 13, 1984.**

Reactions

Against

« A wound right in the heart... that will find its true place in an area known as La Défense... » **Pierre Mazards, *Le Figaro-Newspaper*, May 3, 1985.**

« The Pyramid is a foreign body that does not even have the advantage going for it of being modern. » **Association pour le renouveau du Louvre.**

« A Pyramid is superb in the bareness of the desert, but it would become incongruous in a site to which it is no longer possible to bring significant retouches, so saturated is it with architecture and history already. » **La Demeure historique Association Vieilles Maisons Françaises Association**

« The lost expensive... It cost 50 million francs. That is, it alone has cost half the budget of the total work of renovating the Grand Louvre. Maintaining its 666 sheets of glass will necessitate the acrobatic services of a tribe of Indians imported from Quebec. » **_Le Figaro Magazine_, March 5, 1988.**

« It is too sad to see this project treated from the « management » point of view instead of trying to envision treating it as a poet might, with respect to individuals and artworks.
... The wrong notion is trying to make the underground area the « heart and head » of the Louvre... We don't have to treat it like an airport, after all. » **Michel Guy, former Secretary of State for Culture.**

« Pretty or not, it is absurd. It is presented as modernity. Disliking it, we would have to be like those who deplored the Eiffel Tower. In fact, this Pyramid is behind the times, and for one fundamental reason. The Pyramid does not understand that it has been installed in the center of the Napoleon III courtyard. What exactly is this courtyard, in fact ? The place where the nineteenth century invented what we might call a typically French eclecticism, in a spirit that takes into account the entire stylistic history of the palace. But this Pyramid, in its pure form, belongs to what might be called the great taste for international style architecture, from back in the 1950s. It is completely opposed the entity of the Louvre. You would never think of placing

For

« ... I am not at all hostile to the completion of this Pyramid, considering what I have just seen of it... » **Jacques Chirac, Mayor of Paris, 1985.**

« From the great arch of the Defense to the Bastille Opera, passing by the City of Science at la Villette none of the new Parisian monuments have started as much controversy as the Pyramid. We would have to go back to the construction of the Beaubourg Center, more than ten years ago, to find a similar polemic... » **Rémy Hivroz, _Le Parisien_ Newspaper, April 20, 1988**

« The idea is brilliant... We can hardly be surprised that it should irritate a fistful of specialists whose professional activities orient their glances towards historical criticism rather than towards creation.
... A sculpture made of glass and metal, that in its purity of lines, reanimates the Napoleonic Courtyard... A work of today that breaks with the Second Empire style of the buildings and valorizes the sculpted decorations. A strong historical synthesis... A place for « all the cultures. » **Jean-Pierre Changeux, Professor at the College de France, _Le Monde_ Newspaper, May 15, 1985.**

« What should one think of this project ? At the same time, it is sacrilizing and handily conventional, it will not surprise those who are well acquainted with the architecture of Ieoh Ming Pei, both archeological and modern at the same time. The functionalism is rigorous, the finishings will be impeccable. The lines of the space will be very readable, the symbolic aspect evident and we will be able to read therein a didactic discourse on the piling up of cultures from the twentieth century BC to our modern twentieth century AD. » **Pascaline Cuvelier, _Libération_ Newspaper, January 25, 1984.**

« In the context of the Grand Louvre, it is apparent to the hief curators responsible for the different departments, that the Pyramid of Ieoh Ming Pei that marks the entrance to the Museum, far from being, as it has sometimes been presented, as a fashionable gadget, or a modernist gadget, or at best a gratuitous architectural gesture, is on the contrary a proposition that is perhaps

the Pyramid in the center of the Saint Peter's colonnade in front of the Vatican. Nor would you put it in front of Versailles. You might even think twice before putting it in front of Notre Dame Cathedral.
Paris Mystified, *The Grand Illusion of the Grand Louvre*, by Foucart, Loste, and Schnapper, Julliard 1985.

« The Grand Louvre confuses itself with a Pyramid and an underground forum, posing more problems than it in fact resolves... The important thing in a museum is to speed up the access of art-lovers to the artworks. But this forum, according to the atrocious expression of Mister Pei, has become the « *heart and soul of the Louvre !* »... Ideologically the forum encourages and favorises one of the great weaknesses of our time, that places the discussion of the work over the work itself... The heart and soul of the Louvre are in the artworks themselves. »
Ibid.

« ... We would very much like to believe that the construction of a glass Pyramid in the Napoleonic Courtyard is the result of some sort of contemporary vision. It is certainly fashionable, and the most perfect example that one could give of a post-modernist geegaw... a false pyramid, a simulacrum, a zircon with respect to the claimed diamond it is supposed to be... If it is built, the Pyramid will always seem to be a foreign body with respect to the palace, to the Arc du Carrousel, to the gardens. It will be an element impossible to integrate. It will be one edifice too many. We can only regret the indiscretion and the lack of courtesy that the project shows with respect to the site. The Louvre already has a complete history. This history certainly must continue to be written, but not in this exact same place. But it is here the tip of the iceberg emerges, and the error... another error is in the part of the underground forum, in this immense room of who knows how many wasted steps... that can only retard the public's access to the artworks, and even distract them to the profit of commercial activities, that are subcultural, and whose educative value is far from evident.
André Fermigier, Secretary of the Association for the Renovation of the Louvre, *Le Monde* Newspaper, February 11, 1985.

audacious, but that participates in a complete architectural project that is unanimously appreciated and accepted for its coherence and quality. »
Messrs. Alcouffe, Amiet, de Cenival, Gaborit, Laclotte, Pasquier, and Mademoiselle Bacou, Head Curators of the Louvre Museum.

« ... The project definitively marks Paris, and the history of architecture as well... By the symbol it represents, the Pyramid introduces an architectural continuity, radically reinvented, by the requirements of contemporary thought.
... In utilizing a perennial from completely reinvented, clear in transparency and structure, it proves against all opposition that a secular architecture can be magnified in contemporary architecture. It shows above all how contemporary thought can pursue immemorial quests and still invent, rich with the advantages of yesterday, and even before. So it should always be with visionary architects. »
***Techniques et Architectures* Magazine, September 1988.**

« To apply the word « finished » to the Louvre site seems to me to be unconvincing, for this place that is rather open and incomplete... the architectural additions will stop in a certain year of grace... after which the disgrace will begin... if the « royal deed » only consisted in choosing reputable men known for the excellence of their work, the originality of their contributions, I do not think that we could ever complain about this kind of royalty, let alone about his deeds. In such a choice there is always an element of gambling.
One must always bet on genius. »
Pierre Boulez, composer and conductor.
***Le Matin de Paris* Newspaper, February 15, 1985.**

« ... I have seen the Louvre and its immense precincts, as well as its vast palace which, for two hundred years now is always being completed, and is always being started once again... »
Epigram by Christian VII, King of Denmark, 1768.

What do the French think about it?

A poll conducted in May 1985 when the full-size replica was built.
49 per cent for the Pyramid.
34 per cent against and 27 per cent no opinion.
But 59 per cent of the people questioned admitted never having gone to the Louvre and 50 per cent not knowing what the Pyramid was meant to shelter).
Louis Harris poll for the television station TF1).

Poll completed before the replica, Parisian's opinions.
53 per cent of Parisians for the Pyramid.
21 per cent against and 26 per cent no opinion.
(Poll by IFRESS February, 1985)

Another poll completed in May, 1985 for the Etablissement public du Grand Louvre, at the request of Mr. Biasini :

71 per cent of the people questioned were favorable to the project ot the Grand Louvre.
Based on two thousand responses given spontaneously on the guest books at the Orangerie Museum exhibit in May, 1985 that presented Ieoh Ming Pei's project, these were the results :
86 per cent declared themselves favorable to the project, speaking spontaneously.

The Louvre and How to Use It

Entry : Through the Pyramid, in the Napoleonic Courtyard (principal entryway) ; Richelieu passage and porte Jaujard, (secondary entryways). Metro : Palais-Royal - Musée du Louvre.

The Museum is Open : Every day but Tuesday, from 9 am to 6 pm. Open two nights a week until 9.45 pm ; Monday and Wednesday. Admission Fee : 25 francs. Reduced fee : 13 francs. Free for anyone under eighteen years of age and for the Amis du Louvre.

The Napoleonic Hall is Open : Every day but Tuesday, from 9 am to 10 pm. There is an auditorium, temporary exhibitions, historial galleries, archeologic crypt bookstore, restaurant and café.

Visit-Lectures : lasting ninety minutes. Every day but Tuesday and Sunday. Appointments at the Meeting Place for Groups. General visits, History of the Louvre, visits to one collection, but also more in-depth visits according to a theme, or « one hour, one work. »

The Workshops : Sixty workshops per week. Each lasting about two hours. Sign up at the workshop itself, except for groups, who may reserve places by calling 40.20.51.77.

A Day at the Louvre : Thursdays and Fridays, a program planned with school groups in mind. Reservations necessary. Information sessions for teachers will be arranged as well. For information, call 40.20.51.09.

Groups : Free entry. For the department of Egyptian antiquities and for the services of a lecturer, a reservation is necessary. Call 40.20.51.77.

The Handicapped : Numerous specialized equipment is available for the handicapped, with specific tours scheduled, notably for the blind on Tuesdays. Call for reservations at 40.60.70.64.

Public Orientation : Numerous signboards and video screeens. A guidebook in five languages is distributed free at the entryway beneath the staircase.

Address : Musée du Louvre. 75058 Paris, cedex 01.

Visitors' Information : 40.20.51.51.

Above. Photo Serge Sautereau, fourth level of the roofing.
GEO Magazine, drawing by Pierre Galard.

Publisher J.N. Beyler. Editors-in-Chief : Guy Boyer and Elisabeth Lebovici. Layout by Yoshiho Kirby. Editorial Secretary : Isabelle Duchemin. Published by Beaux-Arts Magazine, a Nuit et Jour Publication, 82 rue Paul-Vaillant Couturier, 92300 Levallois, telephone 47.39.35.35. RCS Nanterre 326 216 389 0014. Employees-Employers Commission 65094. Typeset by Cicero. Printed in Italy.